LAST POEMS

ALSO BY ROY FULLER

Poetry
New and Collected Poems 1934–84
The Individual and his Times: Selected Poems
Subsequent to Summer
Consolations
Available for Dreams
The World Through the Window: Collected Poems for Children

Autobiography
The Strange and the Good
Spanner & Pen

Novels
With My Little Eye
The Second Curtain
Fantasy and Fugue
Image of a Society
The Ruined Boys
The Father's Comedy
The Perfect Fool
My Child, My Sister
The Carnal Island
Stares

Criticism
Owls and Artificers
Professors and Gods

LAST POEMS

Roy Fuller

SINCLAIR-STEVENSON

First published in Great Britain 1993
by Sinclair-Stevenson
an imprint of Reed Consumer Books Limited
Michelin House, 81 Fulham Road, London SW3 6RB
and Auckland, Melbourne, Singapore and Toronto

ISBN: 1 85619 295 4 (h/b)
ISBN: 85619 296 2 (p/b)

A CIP catalogue record for this book
is available at the British Library

Typeset by Rowland Phototypesetting Limited
Bury St Edmunds, Suffolk
Printed and bound in Great Britain by
Clays Limited, St Ives plc

Contents

Preface

In 1985 my father published *New and Collected Poems 1934–84*, an updated version of his 1962 *Collected Poems*. It contained a section of 62 uncollected poems, written since *The Reign of Sparrows* (1980). In the following four years he published three further collections of poems: *Subsequent to Summer* (1985), *Consolations* (1987) and *Available for Dreams* (1989). All these volumes were recognized as an extraordinary autumnal flowering for a poet in his seventies whose daemon had already spoken clearly (as a war poet, for example, and as a poet of deeper mythical or metaphysical themes from the late 1950s). The honesty and humour of these late poems, their intellectual curiosity and their unique ability to tackle sombre human and cultural issues equally with, and in the shadow of, wryly felt intuitions of personal extinction, led readers to make comparisons with Hardy, Yeats or Stevens.

He often said to me, in an odd kind of rueful wonder: 'What shall I do with all these poems I'm writing?' It was as though it were something he could scarcely help, a possible embarrassment to his readers or his publishers. He was far from believing in inspirational mysteries and yet I suspect that privately he may sometimes have been ready for a mood of vocational thanksgiving like that of Rilke at Muzot. He always showed me his poems, but only when they were made up into collections. When, therefore, after his death in September 1991, I came to look through his papers, even I was surprised by the number of uncollected poems which survived him: about 180 typescript pages, and many further poems in eight substantial notebooks used between December 1983 and July 1989. After this date (and particularly after May 1990) I doubt that he wrote any poems other than some new ones for children, although these amounted to a whole new book.

It was immediately obvious that a new and substantial collection was in order, indeed should have been in the pipeline if my father had been able to give it his attention. At its core is the sequence 'Later Sonnets from the Portuguese', written between May and October 1987 and clearly prepared for publication. On the whole I have restricted my choice to the poems which my father had felt good enough to type out, although I have printed a few of those remaining in manuscript. There are about fifteen poems of 1986 or later, i.e. that were too late to be included in *Consolations*, the only one of his last three collections not to be entirely made up of sonnets or quatorzains of some kind. Of the rest, many were written after March 1984, and therefore passed over for *Consolations*, but not thereby necessarily rejected. A remaining eighteen or so I cannot date. I hope that I have chosen the best of the poems that are in clearly finalized form. The business of retrieving all that is of value must be left to a future *Complete Poems*.

This volume is essentially, then, the last of five collections written in just about the same number of years, an extraordinary run of vintages. The fine sonnet sequence in particular stands comparison with the best of his earlier ones, such as 'Mythological Sonnets' or 'The Historian', and its fictional schema provides an interesting contrast with the personal reflections of the other sonnet sequences of the 1980s.

John Fuller

Enigmas

I

Have they constituent parts? How shall we know?
– The particles created in a star,
By us considered weird, ours weird enough.

The sky is cloudless at the end of day,
Graded in colours matched by eggs perhaps
Of common birds. What has it to convey?

According to Heisenberg, even scientists
Shudder before the beautiful – and yet
No wonder, since they see it as equations.

And is the cosmos comprehensible?
I mean intrinsically: some might ask
Even by the Author of its strange inventions.

II

An agitation of the human brain –
Which summons up the ruling principles
Of the universe. Can that be really so?

More likely, many think, a supreme guide
Exists, which matter of all kinds pursues,
However falteringly, through chiliads.

A clock stirs in the quiet house, and measures
The time left (till the final pain and void)
For our divine though wholly earthly pleasures.

I turn a switch. Tunes fill the private night.
The Maharajah did not love in vain
The music of the exiled Muscovite.

III

What is it like to be a bat? It seems
An expert suggests that their experience
Is much like ours. And yes, sometimes the sense

Comes in of flying through the dusk of dreams
Or hanging upside down in dreamless sleep.
And consciousness itself's the strangest thing –

The retina's screen or radar system of
The animal, to which the otherwise
Indifferent atoms have evolved through chance.

– So most maintain, believing time alone
Has made the variously coloured eye,
And patent stow-away umbrella wing.

IV

October snail, do you intend to stay
Motionless on the garden wall, half way
To the top (admittedly less high today)?

For poets, prone to quotidian surprise –
Even behind sophisticated eyes –
Such Tennysonian questions still arise.

Clouds fleetingly make an old nutcracker face,
Behind which, in a quite appropriate place,
A cataracted eye looks out through space.

And does the cosmos somehow hang together –
Suns; replicating matter; autumn weather?
On oceans, jack tars marvel at a feather.

V

Eating black pudding, reading the *Sunday Times* –
Not much to boast about, and yet there comes
An unexpected sense of happiness.

The waning moon, recumbent, glitters through
A neighbour's silhouetted leaves; though, true,
That's also a suburban commonplace.

But what can humans sensibly indite
Besides the science that seems to govern fate?
– Heat up felicity very slowly, lest

The sable gore disintegrate; and stare
As long as patience holds, through earthbound air,
At astral relics of pre-human past.

VI

You hold a newly-minted silver coin.
But is it new, the thing held in the hand,
Being of metal mined from ancient land?

Thus the philosophers see fit to tease:
The riddles trivial, replies long-drawn.
A work of art's a world, said Meyerstein,

That needs no other world to make good sense,
Indeed, can actually in a way explain
This world. I think: how few, remaining days;

Regret for an instant frighteningly intense –
Sensing the silver coin beneath the tongue;
Cycles of song that never will be sung.

VII

Merely a brain (some say) kept in a vat
Of life-preserving fluid, I go out
To night's fantastical phenomena.

Philosophy: the dialogue of far
Divided man, in language, time and space.
Even a kennel has been that palaver's place.

I might well not have ever been – the egg
Fertilized by a different spermatozoon.
And then, would any eyes have turned their view on

A rain-soaked towel hanging from a peg
And, over dark angles of the garden-shed,
The now nude constellations overhead?

VIII

Why does the ice-cube fracture? Once again
Boozing in early evening poses nice
Puzzles. Is it inherent in the meeting

Of solid and alcohol, or the revelation
Of prehistoric layers in the ice-
Compartment's tireless manufacturing?

'Cycles of domesticity and depression' –
I find the phrase applied to Cowper's life,
But few can claim their own much different.

The condensation masquerades as tears,
And runs the ink. November bares its boughs;
The hero having started his long descent.

IX

So what we call the world is merely some
Symbolic construct of a prior mind.
Can anyone believe such sophistry?

A crowd of Johnsonian refutations come.
It sighs down eaves, through supple boughs, the wind,
And oscillates the clothesline in the yard.

Admittedly, critics concentrate too hard
On varying ways of drawing earholes, say –
Neglecting the Crucifixion or Assumption,

The objects of the art. And yes, the state
Of things will never be explained by gumption
Alone. Tempting, to look beyond our fate.

X

And when the plastic crown's cemented in,
The partial plate replaced, the smile will be
A plausible imitation of the truth.

How far such quaint mechanics are from youth!
They've lately found a dinosaur's claw, I see.
Who'd have imagined that its thigh and shin –

Its omnibus-high body – would ever need
To be conjectured from that horny part?
What curious beings must our heirs construct!

Who will suspect we gently kissed and sucked,
Or that our politics and even art
Depended on an ancient power to bleed?

Still-life with Grapefruit

Saturnus loquitur, *not far from his*
Traditional depiction, bent through age
And illness, handling a serpent that bites its tail,
Emblems of the seasons of a year;
Pleased for himself that history records
Even the name of one who long ago
Lobbed horse-dung at the Blessèd Virgin's shrine.

So all they say against me proves the case.
For years I missed the *pizzicato* when
The theme returned. An ancient disc is blamed,
But in reality my nature's slapdash,
Despite its neat exterior. Worse still,
My self-love's of a self I must at last
Admit lacks general interest; proved by this.

Yet, I've just noticed, early in frigid March,
A scaled-down fly on the fly-hued kitchen-sink,
Welcome papa of summer's repellant brood.
To capture the grandeur of the trivial,
Like Seurat! Best to paint a landscape when
The proletariat are not at work,
To guarantee a quite unserious scene.

I'd love to leave, as in Piero's piece,
Foreground enigma in the shape of three
Calm figures, as it were; the theme remote –
The tiny flagellation of a god.
Puzzling triumvirate, though flesh and blood;
Human, and garbed as in the artist's time;
Masks reappearing down the centuries.

Incalculable effects of history!
Gilding an icon in a certain year,
A certain moment in the rise or fall
Of empire, sometimes in its absolute

Kybosh. It shocks me, pondering my rival
Contemporaries, I've never worked my will
On areas entered, of affairs or art.

– Though what the glass returns now contradicts
The puerile follies of its past. Somewhat
Self-consciously, the solo clarinet
Announces its cross-sexual range. What fine
Fellows are those who aim to grow a finer
Fruit than the rest! I render gratitude,
Spooning with ease the tender geometries.

Again the sun shines through the boughs (still bare
However), making patterns on the wall
Beyond my evening chair. Another Spring
Has come; interpretative tasks no more
Facile for being long familiar.
But lucky ancients rub their knobbled hands,
Surviving simply year by unlucky year.

Poem in Three Movements

I

Could Wallace Stevens ever play LPs;
I mean, had he the requisite device?
His letters reperused, the point revives.

Today, the meeting and the dinner, then
Tomorrow nothing more than bake the bread,
And write a passable line or two with luck.

I love the days and weeks when nothing looms,
Save illness and demise. It's in the dusk
That lilies are most conspicuous. You call

Me out to breathe them, too, while through the wide
Window I hear playing on and on
A symphony within a single side.

II

'The chirping fifths' – resourceful phrase from an
Analysis of some work I forget
(As much now, read about in Lethean night),

But surely by no composer of today.
Why do such want the clarinet to sound
So loud and sour? Although quite possibly

Keats-lovers not dissimilarly think
My poetry harsh and unintelligible,
Although it strives for clarity and song.

Must art be always or never out of date?
Music especially often seems time-ruled.
Who would have thought he might survive Glenn Gould?

III

Announce a second subject, that's the way;
As slow and sentimental as you like.
You also get a pattern: A – B – A.

I read (quite obvious when said) that music
Through recapitulation finds its form.
Another trick is near the end to bring

A motif from an earlier movement in,
For choice the most expansive. In the border,
How low the lily dips its triple bloom,

Bowed down, no doubt, by the gold in each corolla.
Tennyson now seems not at all as silly
As Auden thought. Not in melodious gloom.

Duke in Exile

The Duke in exile, trying to escape
From folly's times that fail even to serve
The fools.
                    Along the woodland ride observes
Contiguous, almost circular patterns where
The horsemen passed; and thanks his stars he is
Unalterable in his cowardice.
Forsythia buds hang like a ripe sow's teats –
It's only just philosophizing weather;
Putting great questions underneath the sky.

Wed to a beggar, how is it to end
In the princess's favour? Even if
The spouse were to expire, and thus allow
A marriage to a king, she would have been
Spoilt irretrievably in royal eyes.
It must be that the smelly, ragged fellow
Turns out to be a prince, bewitched; or, like
The Duke himself, testing the pastoral,
The erring or virtuous subjects of his realm.

A warning: buy no gallows flesh, nor sit
At the edge of any well. But who'd pursue
Either bizarre activity? Yet we
May push a door and find a dear one hanging,
Before a nightmare fall into the depths.

There's always a season for unhappiness,
Appropriate or not. The festivals
Of piety or husbandry mark out
The months of pain. His duchess sorely ailed
When the March moon was at its slenderest,
And as his jester went on making jokes.

Still does. But while the greater clowns intrigue
For federated power to start the wars

That will go on until the world is dead,
The ducal clown is consciously a clown;
Knowing of Ovid's exile among the Goths,
Chooses the powerless arboreal court
Where even an equally impuissant sun
Compels the honey-bees, if not mankind,
From still exiguous blossoming begin
A harmless social order once again.

Romance

Brontëan trees, Brontëan skies!
Who wouldn't want to understand
With a novelist's sense of time
Slanting boughs, scurrying exhalations,
Avenging or fated generations –
To sail on to a milder clime
Where love will press a hand
On sightless, once thought scornful eyes?
And who but on a novelist's page
Would have been happy not in youth but age?

Exclamations

Bruno Walter saw Mahler amazingly
As Pan! World of the *Wunderhorn* in stiff
Collars and black frock-coats! Romanticism,

Anyway never less than slightly comic,
Carried on by incurable syphilis;
Madness uncurbed by drugs; and poetry

A by-product of philosophy, e.g.:
'The night is deeper than the day imagines.'
But is the thing less incongruous in our times?

We only have the power to destroy
A movement in a sense destroyed before.
For melody was petering out in works

Commissioned by the other Wittgenstein,
Music and pianist alike deformed
By the first of global battles. Peaceful E

Major, how can it ever sound again?

Coppélia

Among the disseminations of the B
BC, an act of the ballet by Delibes.
The tunes bring back, as though elusive smells,
My youth on piers, in lounges of hotels.

But it has taken sixty years to feel,
Truly, the work's perpetual appeal:
A girl who at her maker's whim can be
Wound up or not for weird activity.

Master Korngold and Mr President

Who can blame brilliant Korngold at fifteen
For Richard Straussian imitation, and
In underlining things with tubular bells –
Even for sounding sometimes like what lay
Far in the future, past exile and war,
Behind *King's Row*, the art that prophesied
A kind of schmaltz would lead the USA?

Minor Keys

I

The mountain spewed; made twenty thousand dead.
But this was merely to anticipate –
For some, less horrid than more usual fate.

But all the draft poems, sketches for finished oils!
– Destroyed by fireballs, under rivers of mud
For ever sunk. Good job the artists died

Ignorant of their loss, Carlylean
Catastrophe only the dotty great could bear;
Or so I think, far from hell's aperture.

II

Sometimes I wish that I had strung together
The meditations of my later life
To make a poor man's *Prelude* or, more like,

Recluse; although the lack of genius counts
Little in nature's cruelty. Indeed,
I feel that once or twice along the road

I somehow got on paper comprehensions
Of rarest emotion, suddenly-seeing eyes,
Aeolian response to melodies.

III

A puddle holds a sky cracked by the season's
Denuding branches: elsewhere in the night,
A moon new-born, though able to stand upright.

Sunlight's a fading yellow in the west.
Just left behind, in Friday's Vanity Fair
Of lighted streets and shops and motor-cars,

The pure yet human beauty of the young –
Still mousiness-unthreatened golden hair,
Responding like some crop to parents' care.

IV

The poet's character: is it any stranger
Than the rest of man's? The predilection for
Puzzles and conjuring; and touching fur . . .

I wonder if it's really morbid, eyeing
Comb-marks and brush-shine. Certainly, very few
Note down such items as that Martinu

Was influenced in 1945
By old-hat Brahms; that Freud preferred to call
His patients 'students'. Am I well or ill?

V

To think of art in the context of disaster!
Already I may have blabbed my secret hope
That, say, in the South Seas Lomaiviti Group

A faithful fan exists who has assembled
My works, and so despite atomic war
They will miraculously pass entire

To the survivors – surely more numerous
Than those on this overcrowded earth who now
Deign to imbibe my sub-Wordsworthian brew.

VI

Leaves having fallen, lit windows reappear
Down vistas from the evening house and lawn.
Voyeurs can see my antics from dusk till dawn.

The pianola proves that even in
(Perhaps especially) the notorious
Prelude Rachmaninov rolled the chords: one must

Be just as moved that Erroll Garner does
The same in the disc of 'Misty'. Random emotion
In a random season – see Uncle Tom's 'Gerontion'.

VII

And yet . . . On the radio I hear a fellow
Articulate the start of Mozart in
G minor, all too often rushed: again

The exploding fire and engulfing mud
Take their subsidiary place, although
Defining where the race of men must go.

Happiness, the final aim of art,
Is always, as we know, too good to last.
How else came minor keys to mean the most?

Summer Laughter

Summer laughter from the gardens
Teases ancient ears.
For the season-ruled potato
The end of scraping nears.

Abundant swell the shapes of summer –
Ridged marrow, pea canoe.
Earth's mighty waters weep like captives
From cucumbers cut through.

Suddenly-ripened berberis berries
By birds' insides are drained,
Blotting the virgin garden benches
With droppings purple-stained.

A thermal whirls a few initial
Leaves in their later coat.
The maestro has to croak in wisdom
Phrases the girl must float.

Hearing Hubert Parry and Beethoven

The consolations of November days:
The individual beauty of the leaf;
A fat fly settling on a whitewashed wall.

How marvellous our moist deciduous lands!
– Breeding an art that sets Shakespearean
Iambics to a simple melody,

Hymnlike and patriotic; and indeed
Once bred the Bard himself. Though in a mood
Induced by the season, that weeps like my old age,

I must admit the violent Kraut expressed
Strange virtue, too – for as the spent sun quits
A yellow sky, above a factory smutch

Of anchored cloud, next from the radio comes
The overture to *Egmont*'s thumb-print, so
To speak: a wrongly poignant piccolo.

Adagios

Utopian, the *adagio*'s calm.
But then Ernst Bloch maintained the art
Itself stemmed from the human sense
That earth could be utopian.

According to philosophy
No hope worth the expression, nor
Dream worth the dreaming ever are
Without the risk of their negation.

Gonzalo spelled his commonwealth
On an isle of music, its creator
Opposing visionary peace
To previous lust and mad ambition.

Maestro

I feel that Ashkenazy sometimes plays
Chopin less well than in far distant days
A master, Mr Tragenza, at my school!
– The Russki perhaps too rapid, as a rule.

I used to hear the little stout austere
Man after prep, and overcame my fear
And sat in the deserted classroom till
He tired or I'd some duty to fulfil.

Two ninnies; or, to speak more generously,
Ships passing, once for all, on life's chill sea.
The gift of music goes with blindness – so
Those who assigned its saint appeared to know.

Dynasties

A work by F. X. Mozart: duly nearer
Franz Schubert than his father, though unlike
Some sons in being stylistically no queerer.

I must say my romantic soul responds
To C. P. E., after old J. C. Bach.
Yet, even here, still strange paternal bonds.

Radio Reverie

I could have seen Busoni; but whose emotion
Is stirred by that nostalgic touch?

– A reverie (Yeatsian word) in which the notion
Occurs that Mozart wrote too much.

And then comes one of many masterworks
From that near-posthumous inspired

Summer – strange benefaction that even lurks
For artists less sublimely fired.

In any case, perhaps we shouldn't too
Much marvel at human genius,

Ourselves being human – Celtish when we're blue;
Remaking Bach as part of us.

Though having heard melody since we were boys
Quit art, and not much in its stead,

Seems little left but *ostinato* noise,
Or the recordings of the dead.

Old Verse, Later Music

The second week in April: first
Moth of the year against the glass;
Return of so universal a burst
Of green as to be ludicrous.

A cat, with frequent shuddering-stops,
Mimics slow-motion film along
The wall . . . 'Whipping their ivory tops'
(I read) 'with golden-twisted thong.'

Now farther from poetic youth
As from the Nineties in that day –
Still farther from poetic truth –
Are things like 'dream-fugues' still OK?

I hear the first of strange Sorabji's
Sonatas for pianoforte –
Indefinite postponement of his
Chords' resolution . . . In life, as art!

Books and Discs

For Eric Walter White on his seventy-fifth birthday

Prokofiev by Prokofiev –
Among a clutch of photographs,
One showing the portly Glazunov
Standing beside a small piano
At which a female child is seated,
Fingers correctly bent on the keyboard,
Straight parting, hair hanging down her back,
Regular profile, far-away look –
Image asexual though erotic
(At least for those of a certain age).
This is Irene Eneri,
Captioned 'A young girl composer' –
She must look now worse than Glazunov then;
Her music even less well-known.
Later, I hear some other music say:
'Bounteous nature never never
Never feels decay.'

Suspicions

Ancient corpses found in Siberian cave –
Poetic headline in *The Times* today.

A good piece, Haydn's Symphony 81
(Catching it on the wireless), but which is not?

Another lucky-dip – a TV spot
Where zapping from the golf to Alice Faye

A foretaste of the pederast's score brings on
A *corps de ballet*, each a glorious girl.

An elegant young vixen visits me
Each evening. No contact. She a nervous sprite,

Her libido only set on food thrown down
To stay her call. So one remains unlovered.

But doubtless any constant love must be
Suspicious as the constant speed of light.

Surely there's some other explanation;
Perhaps a cock-up in the mensuration.

The cosmos has unities yet to be uncovered:
Simple as light, or gibberish, who knows?

Though likely it will always toss its head
And make off, tail at trail or tutu angled.

Any announcement of a four-square theme
Must presuppose a set of variations –

Unpredictable, a few new-fangled.
Where in all this the art-shaped human dream?

– Even the dream of merely being found,
Safe from marauders, mummified underground.

Old American Romantic Films

The past is all in black and white.
Two girls adore the hero, and
One has been blasted by some blight;
The other's loved by Charles-his-friend.

It's perhaps a tumour on the brain
Or (in a concert pianist)
Possibly merely psychic pain,
Dreading notes wrongly struck or missed.

A Jamesian older woman proves
Life finally can be serene,
Even quite comic; and the loves
And illnesses might not have been.

Though death, when sometimes that occurs,
Seems easy – from satin sheets great eyes
Meet other great eyes framed in furs,
Bravely sustaining our great lies.

'Mrs Masters as Hebe'

An eagle meekly drinks at Hebe's hand.
No hint is given by Sir Joshua
Of what old Lemprière called 'the indecent posture'
That cost her the job of cupbearer to the gods.
Mad Blake might well have found significant
So tame a representation. But who can censure
Art for its leniency vis-à-vis
A girl with power to rejuvenate
Not merely the avian and divine but men?

Texts

I open a bible to check a reference:
My God, an overwhelming wealth of phrasing,
Echoing from adolescence and beyond.
But formerly how could I comprehend
Some texts that now leap out at me; for instance
'A time to embrace and a time to refrain from embracing.'

After a Lecture on Rodin
(Raymond Mason)

I shake what strikes me *ex post facto* as
Your sculptor's hand, warm and enveloping,
That like a surgeon's must go everywhere
With love, without fear. And having just been round
The Frenchman's show of clear-cut myriad lines,
My head's full of the human – which you then,
Matching your own art, make more evident.

Below the curls in front of me, the dress
Is cut so as to show one vertebra,
Round which a just-detectable down seems brushed
Quite the wrong way – a mystery not far
From that Rodin investigated: what
Precisely happens in extremest postures
To the appearance of a girl's pudenda.

Returning home, I note the frosty dew
Sparkles on night-time grass as randomly
As stars. And think of Rodin's giant heads,
And your assemblies of the phalanxed crowd,
Your enviable draughtsmanship and his.
No consolation most poets of our time
Depict the simple soul, misshapen, lame.

Prehistory and Post-history

They say it's twice the many million years
Since humans diverged from the apes of Africa
As once was thought – discovery that appears
Of no more moment than that molars may
Have made their crucial changes in Cathay.

Of course, one sees vast time must be allowed
For vegetation-eating mortals to
Digress into an animal-eating crowd –
Threatening not only harmless rumps of blue
But also in the end the green they chew.

Right from the start, malicious denigrations
Were put about of Alexander the Great.
But who the hell cares for warriors' reputations?
One longs to reach a far more ancient date,
And foil the primates' fatal bifurcate.

Humanity's Headache

As Max Born said, it's only possible
To halt, and then perhaps, at best, turn back.

In the small hours an aspirin dissolves –
Time-lapse photography of blossoming.

Or, rather more apposite, slow-motion film
Of dropping a thermonuclear device.

Nasty Weather Ahead

Pollen in peat bogs;
The age of the herring,
Grape-fat years.

Gigantic advance of Alpine glaciers,
Crushing of villages round Chamonix;
Drying out of the once cyclonic Sahara.

The fourteenth and fifteenth centuries –
Dire crises. Then warm winters
Of economic revival, Brazilian gold.

Great thaws, ending of great wars,
After the Sun King's demise.
Who suspected governance by

The circumpolar vortex,
Or minuscule variations
In our axis of rotation?

The future: nothing left on earth
To feel enough terror
At the abrupt return of ice.

The failure of the Gods –
Not to like men.
Thus the failure of man.

Note: The poem is indebted to Emmanuel Le Roy Ladurie's review of H. H. Lamb's *Climate History and the Modern World* (*Times Literary Supplement*, 21 January 1983).

Extinction

Great mammals once were common through the earth.
They must have dreamt as strangely as do I;
Yet not of their extinction. When dreams end –

Anxiously trying to 'phone by touching wires,
After extracting some stupefied relative
From a cab, driven promisingly by

The daughter, that rescued me at the unknown
Station where I'd somehow marooned myself,
By the house of the deficient telephone –

The waking life returns. And thinking of
Extinction, still will stay the frigid space
And universal dust and puzzling force

When life has vanished; as before it came.
Marvelling at the slow-loris pace of dreams
And quite Dickensian waste of incident,

How can I say, even convinced that life's
A sport, I own Liszt's 'bitterness of heart'?
Quite the reverse, in fact, though now grown old,

And notwithstanding that my species seems
Likely to bring an ice-age of its own;
And leaving none to find its teeth and bone.

Voyagers

Voyager 2 is nearing (says *The Times*)
The 'mysterious outer planet Uranus',
Having been on its flight eight years – though that's
No time at all to take to reach the most
Ancient of gods, myself for over more
Than seven decades journeying that way.

Metaphors

The 'golden age' of hell,
The hell of the Baroque –
Billions of bodies mouth
To mouth, amid a stench
Mephitic. From my book
I look up, shocked that some
Experienced in our time
That hell, not just in art
Or under the pulpit's lash,
But on east Europe's plains.

It seems that earthquakes force
Earth to spin faster, through
Compacting it the more –
As skaters faster spin
By tucking in their arms.
The metaphors of man
For the true nature of
The universe must amaze
Even its god. Who dares
To say: incinerate
A chair, and no chair-soul
Can possibly remain?

Ancient Men

Phlegm rattles in the chests of ancient men
Like a door banging remotely in the night,
And just as effectively keeps them awake.

A wet nose serves the sense of smell the best,
Thus to dissolve the airborne molecules.
Primates are dry-nosed; save for ancient men.

Remembering William Empson at a *TLS* Party

The stem grows upright, yet the bulb is skew.
In spite of Empson being some time dead,
The *terza rima* comes to beat anew.

Although its destiny's to end in red,
The pillar reared so far's entirely green.
For critics, meaning is what they have said;

Life's always in the end what must have been.
There are the seasons of the growth and flower,
And other seasons of the quite unseen.

The poets chat at parties for an hour
And then the critics have their longer time.
Remorse can't help but render memory sour:

Its true significance depends on rhyme.
But some maintain the poem as a type
(However it may chime or fail to chime)

Essentially partakes of utter tripe.

Name and Number

Thick buttercuplike April flowers, weeds
In effect: I speculate on what they're called.

'Creeping Jenny' would fit their habit well,
And yet old Keble Martin's marvellous *flora*

Portrays five petals only: these have seven.
Why do we long to learn a name? As boys

Our shyness sometimes attached erroneous names
To girls admired from far. Besides, the months

Of *Lysimachia nummularia*
It seems are June to August . . . by which season

I may well have expired; as yesterday
My friend Charles Johnston, robust, failed to wake

(A letter from me unopened on his mat),
Born later in my year of 1912.

His missus died not long ago: no doubt
His heart was cracked, though held together for

A time, then broke in dreaming of the past.
Nomenclature's mysterious, and likewise

Numbers in nature, more than often odd.
Death picks our lives off, one by random one.

After a Cremation

I.m. AES, 1895–1985

Surely the girl duetists
Will never grow old –
Any more
Than the Gershwin they play.

He's dust in the wind,
The friend who knew my youth,
And saw my earlier follies,
And forgave, like God.

The deity trips from my pen:
The padré revisited, as it were;
Reviving school at prayer
And wind-swept parade-grounds –

Comic or tedious episodes
(The dead himself would agree),
Yet bringing the mind to what's
In the roughly man-shaped box.

Along the *via* to the great age
Of the newly-burned dead,
One comes home, not quite incongruously,
To the inventor of melodies.

What need to admit any death
Except one's own – these days of memories
And of girlhood met in grooves
Unrottable by nature?

The Mysterious East

> For a poet even to have a second-hand
> contact with China is a great matter
> *Letters of Wallace Stevens*

'*A Dictionary of Official Titles in*
Imperial China will be of enormous value,'
Pronounces a reviewer in the *TLS*,
A statement I'm quite prepared to go along with, though
Most likely merely as a general proposition.

But wait a bit. Today I also read that since
Hamlet was first translated into Japanese
In 1875, the Nippon readers had
Upwards of fifty versions from which to choose. Perhaps
Originated really in the orient
The legend in which Claudius bore the name of Feng,
Always suspicious in a Danish context. Hence
The sort of 'welcome home' Shakespeare's reworking gets.

And thinking of my septennate with the BBC,
Learning about MDs, Controllers, Heads of Group –
And not to mention nearly half a century
Seeing my building society proliferate
GMs and AGMs and finer still distinctions –
I wonder if old China may not yet come in.

The Temple Revisited

Marvelling that once I was close myself
To this industrious dark-bodied hive,
I near the foot of Chancery Lane and see
All's much the same, except the newly-scoured
Law Courts, now plainly a wildly comic
Setting for dotty litigants, and Lewis
Carrollian lawyers. Middle Temple Lane
(One of those London hills where brick goes far
To hide the extent and drama of their steeps):
Black-jackets multiply; again I wonder
I matched their know-how in not so far-off days.
I see through casements chunky tomes left out
Like toys, and striped-shirted arms with telephones
Which formerly had me on the other end.
Into Crown Office Row: a curtain
Rises on roses and the Thames. I fear
Surely no less a discontinuance
In England's history than in my life.
The occupants of chambers are painted up –
Names of familiar legal dynasties
And, as seems right, of those with colonial sires,
All, so far, subscribing to the rule of law.
I'm taking tea with friends (he in the past
The tenant of Baconian office in
The Courts); see married life surviving (as
My own does) with threadbare impedimenta
Not worth renewing, precious anyway.
And won't this kind of modus – outside class
Because professional – endure despite
Malaises we three deplore, drinking from cups
Whose courteous scenes our forebears copied from
A culture of more millennia than their own?

Early Retirement

I was bequeathed a second life for song
After escaping from the law, my master;
But used the legacy in a character
That veered between the skinflint and the waster.

It seems my fate was never quite to know
A *modus vivendi* suited to my state –
Except perhaps the felicities of these
Fag-end years, that have almost come too late.

Old Fool

Strange life: a guest at luncheon in the Lords,
Then, before supping on a pizzle of
Black-pudding, hearing Skriabin's clashing chords
That even after years myself have seen
Still pose the question: do we detest or love?
And moving on to Stanford – as though had been
Discovered a not too rotten work by Brahms.

The great arena of the evening sky
Merely contains a trivial moon; conveys
An aircraft lit in maritime attire.
In bed I read of Yeats's faith in fays,
Before succumbing to Temazepams.

Is all now intellectuality?
– We old men standing in a holy fire,
Possessing holiness to nil degree,
The sensual confined to when we sup.

The poet's memory of that 'gazelle':
'I threw the Tarot and the Fool came up,
Which means that nothing at all would happen. I
Turned my mind away.' Today it seems
In some far unimaginable hell
The cards said henceforth life would be drugged dreams.

Prelude to a Party

The lake, half veiled by leafless willows,
Stretches away between the shadows,
Lit by the moon or London's general glare.
Aquatic fowl are roosting on the shore;
Somewhat pathetic dark rotundities.

I feel as though I'm in the Eighteen-nineties;
A world of nocturnes and encounters –
Also, perhaps because of coming down
The spacious ducal stairway, fresh
From tea and toast in the Athenaeum's hush.

The backside of Whitehall, and edifices
Of various religious purposes,
I pass (near at hand
The Houses of the ever tyranny-threatened
Governance of the land),

Bound for a publisher's affair
In unknown Pimlico, wishing that I were
Back home on my suburban height
Where metropolitan decay
As yet has quite to have its way.

Guessing at my host's location,
I turn off by the Army and Navy Store –
Emporium that helped the Empire soar
In some archetypal Colonel's lore)
Above such *fin de siècle* degeneration

As the Rhymers' Club. Red blocks, tall houses loom,
Needless to note, for they must be
Preserved in English Letters – Powell
Or Henry James, the latter already
Giving off a delicate air of doom.

Yet surely those enormous works of art
Escape from History – personification
That's haunted my life, and even plays its part
As I trudge towards my unwished goal
With London Library load, and palpitation.

Friendship

I.m. SHB

An ancient school-friend dies. At least, I hear
About his death in Yorkshire weeks thereafter.
He thought he had rheumatics, but it proved,
As often, that the crab had driven its claws
Too deep to prise apart. Thus ends the career
That started in affection, constant laughter;
Took in a wife, served long in illness, loved;
To me, a life obeying fictive laws.

We left school at sixteen, and never met
From then; he starting writing letters when
We both were sixty-eight: relationship
More doomed than most. His later days were full
Of garden wild-life and the past; and pets
He'd taken on to be a slave again.
He was the last who recalled my famous quips;
And simply couldn't find my memories dull.

What balderdash to asseverate that sex
Lies at the back of all emotion! Yet
I wonder how much his handsome countenance
Persuaded me to love his gentleness.
His last – unfinished – letter will always vex
My memory. That innocent hand was set
In youth, and so seemed to speak its utterance
Across long years; and now the Styx, no less.

In Belfast

In Belfast when the latest 'troubles' seemed
No more than beefs about job-hogging Prods,

I joked among the lawyers and bureaucrats
I'd gone to meet; thought nothing of the stiff

Response. Then not much later I was chilled
To see, on visits for the BBC,

Khaki and guns in red-brick, peacetime streets
That brought my boyhood Oldham back to me,

Mixed with the ghastly endlessness of war.
Once more the relationship of man and art . . .

The foolish male behaviour in the rut!
Some lessons from Rachmaninov and Yeats:

The melody's extension is the thing;
The patience and nerve to drop a rhyme, and choose

A different scheme; or find the inspiration
To flatter a theme with every variation.

You've got to try as long as possible
To keep work secret, for it's never done;

Though in the end one drops it in the stream.
It's said the tunes that go with children's games

Are usually in the major key; unlike
The compositions of Rachmaninov.

In front of houses with no garden ground
The happy voices rise to Queen or Mary,

Before sectarian glands bring throbbing wounds.

Late Meeting

I say to my companions in the car:
'The City's at its best this witching hour' –
The northern sky still light
But office windows bright
In up-ended boxes that absurdly tower
Over the previous roofs of work and prayer.

Returning, astonished it should subjugate
The lamps, I see the moon illuminate
The bridge's massive iron,
Clearly perhaps as when
Intrepid Victorians deftly turned the nuts
On the gigantic bolts, and rigged the struts.

I read once that before the Romans there
Was no London. Possibly in the air
Above the serpent river,
Just fordable, a quiver
Of subsequent glass and concrete, domes and spires,
Perturbed the prophets among our ancient sires.

The limousine crosses the former turbid lakes,
Formerly flooded at high tide. The dykes
Are now enormous arches
Preventing return of marshes.
Though Togodumnus died, we must remember
The British could not be forced into surrender.

To what but craft and language do we owe
Allegiance now? I ponder, as I go
To disputatious Kent,
What history has meant
To islanders at the mercy of the seas,
Their weather loathed and loved by vandal prows.

In youth I lived almost beyond the reach
Of Romans, the culture and war they had to teach.
It's my own history
Has strangely transported me
Into this world of beetling layers raised
On Queen Boudicca's scorched and levelled waste.

Pig-lag

Tricky circadian rhythms youth ignored!
But now hot bottles must sustain by night
Toes' temperature, and diuretic pills
The euphemistic waterworks by day.

It seems the pig is equally vulnerable:
In artificial night and day its normal
Responses soon break down, and it becomes
A case of heavy jet-lag, so to say.

– No wonder, having been associated
More than nine thousand years with humankind:
Man's fellow feeling in old age may well
Have helped it on its domesticated way.

On the Way to the Compost Heap

On the way to the compost heap a field mouse
Lies in my path, its throat torn out,
A werewolf's victim. Never much aware

Of such small deer as part of secret life,
Even in moonlight, reminded by the owl,
I now conduct the gravest episode

Of its existence on our star –
An ill-equipped mortician, fearful of bodies,
And not just the bodies of the dead.

Yet despite pity and distaste,
That forces everything to be done in haste,
I note the neat brown habit, blood red as berries,

Tail worthy of evolution's aeons.
And after the spade has done its work –
Grave-digger and detached pall-bearer, both –

I wish I'd had the guts to scrutinize
The corpse, and so find further metaphors.
For what? For life or death, who knows?

And, after all, must the burial of love
Imply a severance of the head,
However devastating seem the blows?

Turds and Guts

Am I reduced to setting in a verse
A fox's turds? (I think disparagingly.)
These nonetheless are not unnotable,
Being like dogs', of chalky consistency.

Maybe they are some hound's, that leapt the wall
During a Baskervillean *nocturne*.
Even insomniacs can't keep in view
All that goes on beside a garden urn.

Superfluous such musings, as I see,
Preparing lunch, a herring's silver gut;
Confirming that what's wonderful is less
The naming than the thing itself, however put.

Autumnal Fires

I save a spider from the fire;
Dream of old colleagues, whether dead
Or alive indifferently.

But down what years has gone desire?
Why don't I mourn what's wholly fled?
It merely seems to me

A marvel that man and brute inspire
Preoccupation in a head
So far from carnality.

Philosophy in Marks and Spencer

To be alive! Astonishing state of matter –
Inherently, let alone at seventy-four.
And yet I ponder whether or not to buy
A two-pack of vests, singles for sale no more.

A wardrobe in the face of death is like
Some nerve-racking game of cards in which to win
One must end with as few as possible.
And surely this comic vacillation in

A way bears out my firmly-held suspicion
That freakish in the universe, perhaps
Unique, is what can reproduce before
Decay, such as old, stingy, one-vest chaps.

Musicology in Safeway

with thanks to Arnold Whittall

I see an old fellow clutch and contemplate
A carton of eggs, and well appreciate
The doubts that make him so long hesitate.

The price is printed not too legibly,
The ovoids' size and even integrity
Unclear, though cased in patent transparency.

I read a bold musicologist has stated
That once the dissonance was emancipated
A consonance need not be designated.

And Bartók thought that music might be freed –
An oppressive hierarchy displaced, indeed,
By symmetry: eggs spread according to need.

But how can such utopian extremes
Still animate us ancient fellows' dreams,
Moved as we are by diatonic themes?

At the Supermarket Checkout

At the supermarket checkout
Stranger than usual purchases
Before me on the conveyor-belt:
Cartons of buttermilk;
Digestif Rennies;
A circular tin of Danish sprats.

I glance up at the purchaser:
Sure enough, Chekhovian characteristics –
Specs, greying locks untidy at the back;
No receptacle for his purchases;
Bewildered air; mind on menaced
Forests of birch, or cholera in Yalta.

Only dragging my own goods home,
As a moujik with a sleigh, do I ponder
What literary allusions may
Have occurred to him.

Scrag-end

Under the apple-tree,
On an invisible string,
A living grub revolves –
Some mystery of Spring.

Contrariwise, how much
One knows is usually
Missing, even from
Quotidian poetry –

In stews, scrag-end of lamb,
Its gnarled bones that inlay
The tenderest of the meat
And also (but what are they?)

Fairy pillow-shapes,
Yellow, inedible.
As carefully as a thread
From my own eye, I pull

To safer air the dangling
Wriggler. Strange, I am
Far less concerned about
The life-blood of the lamb.

Surprised by Spring

Even indifferent gardeners must surprise
The garden's owner, after their demise,
By what successive seasons cause to rise.

These bits of blue and yellow touch even me,
Who put them in the earth; at seventy-three
Surprised by what I half thought not to see.

Family Christmas

I

The cat's so agèd that she now appears
Only towards our visit's end. And we
In human terms possess as many years;

And must seem equally withdrawn to those
To whom the crux of abdication from
The world of matter has been scarcely posed.

The river makes for empty boughs a glass;
Beside it, the colour of both snow and slush,
Cygnets, like Nebuchadnezzar, eating grass.

II

It's taken me till I was short of breath
To recognize A minor – so I think,
Back home, a work of usual life-in-death

By Schubert occupying Radio 3
(I left behind a present of the score
Of Mendelssohn's quartet in that same key –

The precocious boy apparently having seen
Beethoven's recent Opus 132).
One breaks a naked twig and finds it green.

The Book says: 'Tell thy servants the dream and we
Will show the interpretation'. Sometimes art's
Like Babylonian astrology.

In April

In April, long enured
To early dark, we are
Amazed how late the noise
Of outdoor life goes on.

A blackbird has been lured
To sing before a star;
A distant shout from boys
Some mower's antiphon.

In the Shed

A whorl (buff, papery, shell-like) in the shed,
Enclosing a set of tiny hexagons;
The whole affair, like some strange orthopod,
Adhering to the inside of a hat –
Spare gardening lid, unused for many moons.
Baffled initially, as though had lit
And found this dwellinghouse's secret core
Spermatozoa from another star,
I quite soon recognize the art of wasp;
Really almost within our earthly grasp.

Difficult Distinctions

'Distressingly difficult genitalia':
The phrase encountered in the *TLS*
Proves to relate to *Lepidoptera*
Not *Homo sapiens* as one might guess.

In the same piece I'm pleased to find out there's
No easy way to tell moths from butterflies –
Less guilty at the fluttering affairs
That baffle naming under transient skies.

And So Forth

The spiders, snails, woodlice, and so forth
Don't seem at all pleased that I'm clearing out
The slums of the ivy on the garden wall:
Rubbishy cobwebs, leaves of anterior autumns.
The spiders scuttle, some as white as ghosts,
Some globular but agile, youthful fatties.
The snails emerge from shelldom, uniformly
Ectoplasmic, horns and all.

The ivy itself has grown – how has it grown?
Worn-hairbrush roots revealed, nourished on
Exiguous Victorian mortar.
The interested birds look relatively
New, though one knows they waited like this
Long before man provided the bounty.

Old habitations – like our own
Carpets and mattresses and so forth,
That need renewal for another
Forty-odd years of marriage – 'years' understood
In our hearts as centuries, millennia!

Advice to the Elderly

Like November's great blue fly,
If the day is mild go forth,
Though the sole blossom (of
The ivy) a mere green pseudo-flower.

Keep house contentedly
Should the April wind stay north:
What will come your way of love
Now past the exercise of power.

Gulls over the Capitol

An alien wing or two among the gulls
That paper the heath, perhaps flown newly down
From Scandinavia – beyond! – where winter
Crystals already mass for their blockade.
Even allowing for his theft of fur
And fire, how can man compete with birds?

Balakirev used to consult a female seer
On Nikolaevskaya Street. Quite young, with large
Dark eyes, she looked into a mirror where
Persons appeared whose thoughts she read, then told
Her clients. The composer sought the fate
Of some projected concerts, and his war
Against the detested Russian Musical
Society.
            Petersburg before its end!
I see the gulls departing from the Neva –
From Revolutions, from the Nazi siege –
As when it suits them also will depart
From our own unpredictable bourgeois weather.

Best and Worst

O myriad drugs, enabling humankind
To conquer the travail of insomnia,
Acidity, anxiety, even pain!
How could we bear our lives in times before
Chemists' contrivances, animals' sacrifice?
– Though every generation will put the case,
Even beneath barbarian invaders
Or home-grown maniac, since few accept
Things in the long run really can get worse.
Days of fermented liquor, simples plucked
By moonlight in Titania-haunted woods –
Life always looked both ways: to old brute brows,
Future laboratories, fatal in the end.

The Envious Poet

Even as I swallow a crimson tablet of erythromycin
To kill the cohorts of evil invading my chest, I feel
Regret that I must leave to painters and composers
Areas of art I've always longed myself to fill,
Although about to quit my own art unfulfilled.
I see that to depict the trailing foreground of leaves
You let the dark-green dry before applying light,
And that the quality of melody is even
More vital for success in quick parts than in slow.
But what to do about it with these wheezing words
Would take another lifetime to sort out, to say
Nothing of needing a more capacious pair of lungs
That easily would range from deep bassoon to white.

Triangles

I dream you've left me; wake, and find you gone.
The dream was of a rival, falling out
Of love, an anguish terrible to bear.
Waking is almost a relief – to know
We're old, so old such triangles must be
Quite ludicrously far into the past;
And if there's a rival he bears a common name
And merely sits beside you in the ward.

First and Last Loves

To chance or contrive, as a boy,
To sit by a girl (in a car,
Perhaps) – an excitement far
From simply sexual joy.

Yet certainly such event
Was underwritten by
The forthcoming power to try
To make man permanent.

And stubborn loves for the worst
In womanhood succeed
The shy but urgent need,
The frail, idealized first.

In old age come again
Those fleeting amours; but now
Neither time nor flesh allow
A future of lasting pain.

The Letter

I see from the envelope
Your fingers formed my name –
The personal row of letters
Written by those new carrots
Ending in gnawed-at horn.

Nothing more intimate
May be expected after
The envelope is slit –
From the epistle's subscription
Nor its assignation.

Venus, Mars and Cupid

To rub the pane and startle Venus, apart
On navy-blue, and in the electric blur
Divine her actual phase! This month the star
Pursues and even catches gory Mars.

I dozed off earlier in the day, my dreams
Making their fresh arrangements of the past:
My son, escaping nude as Cupid from
His bath, before the war that severed us.

How soon, my standing in the holy fire,
Far from the consequences of desire!

Late Movie on TV

Not quite unfuddled, to be sure,
I weep at the great art-passion of
My long existence, in miniature.

Drowning, my own life flashes before
Me – paying no heed to mother-love . . .
A glorious girl . . . absurd old bore.

February 12, 1912

The morrow of my very day of birth:
End of the Manchu dynasty,
After two hundred and umpteen years.

P'u-i, boy emperor, resigns his power
(Merely by edict his descent
From the Empress-Dowager).

And a baby emperor appears –
Whose reign is shorter still.

Even had my siblings not arrived,
Would omnipotence soon
Been forced to abdicate?

Lost, the great breast of China;
Never but briefly possessed
The father's territory.

February 11th

The champagne for my birthday
Need only stand outside
For it to numb the palate
An instant, as required.

Even as glasses are lifted
I think back seventy years:
The Failsworth house-pipes frozen;
My mother's hopes and fears.

The Years

Twenty-two years go by: again Mark Gerson
Arrives to photograph my bardic person,
One day in winter; brings a print that he
Arrested time with in 1963.

I'm on a garden-seat – the wood it's made
Of since renewed (and once again decayed).
A fag burns in my hand – first thing I see:
A pleasure I renounced in '73.

Despite young looks, it's plain I'm slightly ill:
The gland's toxicity undetected still.
The twigs are swollen, like those I'll be alive
(It seems) to sit beneath in '85.

Amazing Night

Amazing night – but then most nights amaze
If old age troubles to venture out of doors.
Even one night of a great moon close to Mars
Might well cheer up his residue of days.

Bad luck, though, if after one night of that sky
He dies in moonlight sleep, his slippers dry.

Aubade

Actions on waking: inserting some upper teeth;
Washing down water-pills with what remains
Of water from the night's Sahara; socks

Achieved with grunting; specs slipped in a gown
Assumed like Caesar's for the fatal Ides;
Seeking *The Times* beneath the letter-box;

Bisecting a grapefruit; frying a cold potato
With egg or bacon, even both, for greed
Sharpens in age. And thanking what Gods there are.

To plough through the prosaic to poetry –
The only way of versing that I know.
The life so simple, the dreaming so bizarre.

Almost unguilty Nibelungs fabricate
A frightful armoury for maniacs,
As unforeseen as once were Hitler's packs;

And men will come across the poisoned bait
And eat it up – because of history
And time, forgetting they laid it down themselves.

Outside, goldfinches cling to thistle-heads,
Reckless of hurt – black-spotted tail, the poll
Black-spotted, too, over Renaissance red,

The gold along each pinion's leading-edge.
Mankind's sole purpose is to live beside
The extravagance of species, itself a freak

Of quite indifferent chemistry and chance.
Scriabin's *Mysterium* was to last a week,
Involve all the arts, transform the human race.

The music of Scriabin formed the new
Back in my childhood, so is it really true
A plangent stream has run into the sand

Or was the range of hearing frozen then?
The severed fruit lies Danaë to the gaze,
And, thinking of the geography involved,

It could be Jordan's water in the spoon,
Baptising tongue with tart deliciousness,
That organ having learnt to compensate

For the palate's masking by the plastic plate.
And as to that it seems the blood soon lines
The tubes of orlon (inserted to repair

The body's vessels) with a vascular
Endothelium, like the real thing.
No wonder with false-teeth one still can sing.

Conveniently, a hand fits in a shoe
Taking a polish-laden brush. But few
Seem to tread leather in this orlon age,

Let alone bother to keep it bright – save those
Perhaps touched merely with water, still awaiting
The spirit; and are yet so close to death.

Still, who would wish Arcadia to be free
Of its Inhabitant? For only scythe
And hour-glass free it from triviality.

My Life

Soon, no one will remember my eccentricity –
A fair example, fitting 'Oh Dearie me today'
(The catchphrase of a childhood landlady)
To the tune of 'Lady Be Good'.
And who else will echo my grandfather's phrase
Of assent when offered a second helping:
'Just for amusement'.

The hairy torso has collapsed beneath
The somewhat less than right-angles
Of the octodic legs.
Spider, art tha sleeping there below,
Or dead? Perhaps it may come to be said:
He was a man who used to care about
Intruders from another world.

I see my life's immense alternative –
Wife dead in childbirth (as she nearly was)
And I in the ensuing war with thus
Less motive to try to save myself from the worst.
As it is, I'm older than my grandfather,
And most days making fresh discoveries –
That Rimsky wrote Rachmaninovian songs;
How martins gather under a sky of greys;
And down a garden wall a snail
Moves rather quicker than a minute-hand.

The Story

Most of the inconveniences of my
Demise will not, however, be borne by me –
Consoling, now that almost anything
Unusual brings with it anxiety.

Often I feel perhaps I don't mind death –
Still free from pain and lameness, despite old age;
And yet I blench to think some moment in
The story I shan't be there to turn the page.

Later Sonnets from the Portuguese

Beholding, besides love, the end of love . . .
EBB

I

The poet watches fat beneath the grill
Blister from white to brown, a quantum shift
Reminding her of Nagasaki's skin.

One of her bread loaves sticks: a bit is left
Behind – a jigsaw piece she must detach
And turn to fit in the appropriate hole.

Weeding a bed, she discoveres broken glass
From a war she hardly witnessed. Why not be
The fifth or sixth to write 'vastidity'?

She wants the world to be more like herself;
Yet, copying any corporal, files her cans
In ranks of size upon a kitchen shelf.

And takes a book up when chores cease to press:
Shaxberd's *Mesur for Mesur* in modern dress.

II

Fatherless children, poems – more or less.
Her natural progeny in crueller ways
Were orphans. Tears well up; she dabs the cambric.
The slumbering cat reminds her of the days
When suddenly a noisy child slept thus
(Odd moment, deathly sleep) and she was free
To write of the Permian catastrophe
Or, say, pre-Cambrian times – assorted tripe
Miraculously blending into verse.
But who knows when inspiration's over-ripe,
If time must make the poet's language worse

As it inevitably brings the placid?
O great deoxyribonucleic acid!
– Even the molecule of life's iambic.

III

Rulers and sexual partners in disguise –
Foreshadowing the Vienna of later days,
Freud added to its 'timeless monuments'.
She looks up from the ingenious final wonders
Of reconciliatory transference;
And not entirely incongruously ponders
How long since she felt the fuzz and amazing warmth
Of unclosed skull against her open mouth.

As in the case of comradeship and war,
Of motherhood the memory retains
Only felicity. Outside, a pair
(Content upon a bough) of collared doves –
The number of happiness in diverse loves
It well may be she'll never know again.

IV

The elder bushes emanate their being
From fleurets mainly greenly beaded still
(Full foam to come), like waves far off from shore.
Surely she must have versified before
The catspee scent, just as she's always seeing
A blackbird's angry downturn to its bill.

'He hath but as offended in a dream'
– The words remind us that the work is set
In Freud's own city. How extraordinary that
Not only human dreams but human lives
Are acted out amid both canvas trees
And things that are quite simply what they seem.

Empires and schools of melody today!
– Only the pastoral resists decay.

V

Undoubtedly offputting, those extrusions,
Resembling the body's interiority;
In some moods she wants easier illusions –
Perhaps platonic nights . . . or even years.

Sayings of lovers: You are like a fox,
Smaller than I imagined. And then harking
Back to affairs before they even met –
Opposite poles of verse and jealousy.

A sudden shower: the slanted roof-tops smoking
Beyond the blue and exhaled grey of his.
The masculine – almost too crude to stand,
And yet she stood it, as do all her sex.

Jack Palance in the movie, *Chato's Land*,
Avowed: 'We stay till the 'pache breed is hung'.

VI

Unfortunate, the anguished botheration
Of parting should coincide with inspiration,
When often in art life's commonplaces tell.

The starling's body now is almost gone,
Ravaged by flies and ants, and saving her
Distasteful offices of burial.

The universe is young, or so aver
Fashionable astronomers – less than
A dozen gigayears. So what's to come
May yet outgrow these really quite insane
Contingencies of flesh and blood and brain;
And, singing voices made for ever dumb,
The cosmos settle exclusively to nice
Or wildly unstable packets of fire and ice.

VII

It's early summer: in the garden tree
Green embryo apples have uncannily
Appeared, in somewhat science-fiction mode –
Invaders from outer space that must assume
Organic forms to prosper on the Earth.

Her daughter was determined to be born;
Precaution, steel, mandragora, evil stars
Proving quite powerless to prevent the birth.
How infinitely reassuring, the force
Of tiny seed – of infancy, and youth!

She all at once seems to see the truth of things
(Slicing tomatoes with a saw-edged knife).
O fly, escape to other flies! She flings
The window open, as though upon her life.

VIII

A spider dreams away the day and night
Below the clothesline, just beyond the pane.
Various beasts squeeze underneath the screen
That marks the boundary of her back domain
(A vanishing ambiguous tail is seen) –
Area illumined by the kitchen light.

The spectral moonbeams fill the silent house;
Vanished the whimpering brood and snoring spouse.
It's almost as though her years had never gone,
And she feels ready once more to take on
The making of a unit in the nation;
Though the small hours show her habitation
Shared only with such as silverfish. The ridge
Of background snow is freezer piled on fridge.

IX

The Duke (she thinks), no less than Angelo
And Isabella, apt analysand
Of Freud in the later city. What deep woe
Carlylean wisdom may conceal! The banned
Desires – one upright furrow in the brow.
No purgative, not rhubarb nor yet senna,
Can rid her of memories that make her now
Merely 'a looker-on here in Vienna' –
The actors in the drama of her days
Gone forth to take the lead in other plays.

Could she live on if passing eyes ignored
The outward form presented them to see
(Beauty she owned so long it almost bored)?
And yet they do that thing; and so does she.

X

Her father and his politics came from times
Surely of more illusions than her own,
Rather as her children's folly seems
Folly to her and little else. Between
Those who released the atom and those who now
Appear forgetful of it, she exists,
Appropriately middle-aged. But how
Unfit she'd be to inhabit either era!

Chicks seem enormous once they've left their nests.
After his heroic years the father
Shrinks. In this stretch of life, mere passing showers
Confine her to her solitary room.
Almost as good to visualize the flowers
As live through the week or two until they bloom.

XI

To her surprise she saw his poetry
Develop – seemingly having thought herself,
Not least in parting, the one essential Muse.

So winter went and summer again came by:
No more the garden a background for the wolf;
Lavender was vibrated by the bees;

Three mushrooms sprouted on her unmown lawn.
She wishes she could always have been free
To say: 'Nothing repels me.' But, of course,
Even in their relation's rosy dawn
The seasons revolved, and (imperceptibly
At first) time changed things, as it does, for worse.

And just for the bombus, nature, after all,
Goes to some trouble to set out her stall.

XII

She struck 'amreeta' out as too *outré* –
As though his critical regard were still
Over her shoulder. Can there come a day
When what has been has no great part to play?

And yet it seems not long ago her will
Controlled the future by being dominant
Over the present. Already quite a fossil,
She now sees youth short-sighted as the ant.

You have to live through a morbid lust for words,
And try to write the truth of being down,
And take the cracked potato with the sound –
For as she cogitates, some begging birds
Light on the kitchen window-sill, their brown
Eyes on the potato-peeler in her hand.

XIII

In fact she never missed home-talk and blessing
And the common kiss. New vistas of walls and floors
At once supplanted what she might be missing –
As though she had grown up with dark-green doors,
High ceilings, of a Victorian maisonette;

One adored male, and not a varied shoal
Of sexes, ages, love. And so the set
Of sequent homes, improving, on the whole.
Thus she is left with empty rooms as well
As empty hours. It's only where a knife
Pares parsnips or potatoes she can quell
Her domicile's unintelligible fears.
You switch the light on and a moth appears,
To look in through the window on your life.

XIV

Man is a primate foetus that's become
Through chance of ages sexually mature.
After her bath she ponders the human frame:
Science is not quite sure what nails are for.
Is it her future for no one to care
About her body and its destiny?
Even herself seems somewhat cavalier
As to its tie-up with the essential she;
Though should some peninsula of pain occur
She'd only be too concerned to cut it free.
Quite wolfish, what the scissors make to trim;
May grow the more so as the years advance;
Hands, too, become less assiduous to proclaim
From the wild kingdoms their profound difference.

XV

Her father thought that politics comprised
The quick of living in our modern day;
And so when she grew up she was amazed
To find someone she loved for whom the word,
The phrase, the paragraph, were really play,
And could be as nonsensical as a bird.

Anxiety about far-off régimes,
And whether history is saying alas,
All at once lifted. And arrived the times
When private language seemed an esperanto;

And heroine and hero fell to assess
Themselves in canto after ample canto.
It was as though a voice was speaking: whose
Rule, Fairie Queene's or Blatant Beast's? You choose.

XVI

O frail original and faded bliss,
Faded in retrospect so soon, if not
As quickly diagnosed fundamentally frail!
And while that dwindled, his reputation grew
Not least because that famous work of his
Delineated the emotions hot
From two bound close, from labiate head to tail;
And she herself engendering what was new.

Unlike the Chinese, frogs are really all
The same (or so she reads). Batrachian,
The facts of love – though there speaks middle-age,
Blasé because no longer can befall
Lips breathing on the face like a scented fan,
Or pressing their crimson imprint on the page.

XVII

The wild flower chooses where it best may thrive:
Not always where it's difficult to pick,
For its abundance seems meant to heal the sick.
And man is helped agreeably to survive
By nursing spiky parsley, lengthy chive.
Anticipated like a nervous tic,
The bar of the tune where the drummer drops his stick,
Too amply proving the recording live.

Nature and art: the metaphors in each
At last quite overwhelmed her, whereas he
Was able in these disciplines to teach
The young, and in their compost-flattery
Grew fat and sleek and languid as a leech.
Who's the true sonneteer then, he or she?

XVIII

And as for her, fame turned (to match her themes)
Domesticated; house-bound as a cat.
When her affections were at large, it seems
Her conquest of the youthful literate
Was effortless, complete. No more, no more!
Now she writes only of the fatal flaw
That clatters round regularly, as it were,
Among the improvisatory, to gnaw
The memory with remorse. He moved away
To match his audience with lovers, eloped
To cities she'd never visit, where the day
Was rich with the compost of the night. She hoped
Merely to go on showing existence as
A beetle world deep hidden in the grass.

XIX

Windings of dark acacia boughs, among
Their stippled green – yes, but what metaphors
Can nature lend when love's gone badly wrong,
And living's channelled in its narrowest course:
Mere breathing, eating, sleep (not much of that)?
And what a daunting amplitude of hours
She finds she suddenly possesses, sat
Surrounded by unemblematic flowers
(Although on an acacia bough a dove,
Rather too aptly deserted, squats like her).
Yet she surprisingly wouldn't in a way
Want to re-live her life, neither before
Nor after she was vitalized by love –
Almost repelled by her vanished stamina.

XX

Her outdoors mug of tea steams into sunlight
Angled and partially obstructed, like
(She fancies) a street-lamp filtered through a fanlight.
And does the rhyme-word make the matter true,

Life justified by noting for noting's sake –
As, the inimitable damson hue?
Nearly in secret, the habit of poetry
Went on; was then uncovered, so to say,
By time, and now stands steaming in a cup.
It did not turn in her, 'the thing called love',
To hatred, though that emotion doubtless drove
Him from the house where children had grown up –
Who played among the trees that shaft the sun
In a strange summer of being the only one.

XXI

She used to read from a collected Grimm
To offspring who perhaps were mesmerized
Less by the stories than her voice, and dim
Light and the weariness from play. Good thing:
For often she found that she was uttering
What would have hurt them had they realized
Its import – like Joringel, whose Jorinda
Was changed to a nightingale for ever more,
The culprit an old witch with yellow skin.
Ah, days when she could think herself a part
Of song and sadness, yet with nothing to hinder
Her closing the cruel book and bedroom door,
Leaving a kiss above each tiny chin,
To join the faithful Joringel of her heart.

XXII

Call it ironic that as she lost her beauty
(Prompting him to gaze – elsewhere – the more),
The children's love was damped, then turned to duty;
The relation scarcely better than before.
She thought: my role is changing to the witch,
Who changed the girl into a nightingale.
How long before she becomes a cat or bitch;
And existence cruel, like a fairy tale,
And as unlikely? With spider, moth and mouse,
She sees the full moon shining all the night

Into the now far too commodious house,
And so the opposing panes in turn ignite.
Perhaps it would not have needed the traumatic
To demonstrate her place was in the attic.

XXIII

It seems a last-century medico maintained
That women's reproductive cycle and
The organs of reproduction themselves inclined

The sex to lunacy. One remedy
(No doubt of quite short-term efficiency):
A vulva packed with ice (if that could be).

But apathy, listlessness and inanition –
The classic symptom-cluster of depression –
Who's to pontificate on their causation?

Such act of mourning is a vain revenge,
Since the revengee's then long out of range,
Gone to a sane if over-heated change –

A pale young face in tangled yellow hair,
Clothes that just sketch her as already bare.

XXIV

Its incandescence lights the window-frame,
Then falls indoors upon the rocking-horse
They kept on sentimentally in the room
For long a nursery. She wandered in
(She tells herself) to see the spectral moon
From this now empty quarter of the house.

The forty-four elaborate protocols
Of love were easily within her power
Even in days of steeplechasing toys.
In fact, she felt her vision brooding over
Europe, its millions familiar as the dolls
That populated the present ghostly place.

Now she looks up enviously on this eye
That tirelessly views all stuff beneath the sky.

XXV

Illyria, the girl was living in –
Sadness of morning brothers; ludicrous sadness
Of thwarted ambition tending near to madness;
Sadness of clowning, of being daft and thin;
And yet perhaps was always a suspicion
That things would work out happily some day,
At least for the chief *dramatis personae*,
With whom she was numbered in her secret vision.

Yes, life showed itself a comedy, despite
The Learish father, and suspenseful Acts
Before the astounded, unlikely, happy greetings.
But, looking back, whose would be now the right
Collected volume to enshrine the facts,
The play proving not to end in lovers' meetings?

XXVI

She was amazed when one day, one specific
Day, showed his love for her had gone – in fact,
Changed to disliking almost as terrific
As once had been the feeling it replaced.
She never considered then that she had lacked
At times, across the years, the constancy
Of ardour that alone could justify
(It might be said) the extent she was amazed.

Emotion makes one's head ache, she thought after.
The solitary tears did not come back:
Instead, a constant unanticipation
Of joy fell on her; no exaggeration
To say like one on Death Row or the rack;
Affecting even the return of laughter.

XXVII

Sleeping prefers the proxy of the wish
And not the evil wish itself, like art.
It jibes, that she was once a dozy bard.
Then came the cobweb-breaking, wakening kiss.

It was as though another father had
Appeared, so how was she to know at first
A war was pending; so to speak, the fists
Of rival sons – two from the primal horde?

Love loves to swear to last until – beyond! –
The grave, and, if not, then falls short of love.
Though who need swear for ever to be fond
Of issue? As for them, they merely strive
In curious ways to go on loving those
They hugged with freedom in primeval days.

XXVIII

In dewy mornings she takes up her pen.
The damsons come and go, and after all
Their crimson stain proves not indelible.
She'll leave behind her in her *oeuvre* – and *vie*! –
Trace of the 'primal insatiability'
Of her desires; or so she hopes. But then,
What novelty? For common to all human,
The loss of being once a part of woman;
And that she has indeed bequeathed already.
Against her face the evenings now are thready
With webs – between the outhouse and the line,
Outhouse and damson-tree incarnadine.
The corner-loving spider in this season
Sits in the centre of its spangled reason.

XXIX

Putting dried peas to steep, one pea pops up:
A poet, a freak from a contented mass –
Content to be drowned and tenderized and at last

Devoured. But this (part brown, a half-size pup)
Makes as to escape its siblings' destiny.
Of course, now she could wish that when he kissed
Initially he had, as it might be, missed.
Her sex at first is inclined to acquiesce
When faced with pouring, hot emotion, just
As the pea-consensus. And when apparently –
Years later, that seemed a dreaming quickly passed –
His passion changed to hatred, once again
She could do little, like the chimpanzee
Who quite lacked grammar, though had learnt to sign.

XXX

She ducks the webs like a boxer, and feels sad
When sensing an alien thread among her hair
At dusk. If only all the animal –
And human – kingdom had such respect for right!

But plainly the Primal Cause built in the bad.
And she herself is conscious that in her
Are both the timid scuttling and the evil
Of binding and sucking dry the free in flight.

Entering the night-time kitchen she has seen
The cooker's pilot-light's mysterious glow,
And then perceived that even the washing-up
Possessed its worlds of supernatural sheen.
Past bitterness, the draining of a cup –
Simplicity of all that we can know.

XXXI

Occasionally he sadly wept as well.
Tears of the crocodile, she thought, and may
Even have said. If so, no wonder they
Are living he in heaven, she in hell.
Or, rather, she assumes his happiness,
Exaggerates her misery. Of course,
It was no lack of sympathy in the head

(Which speaks and takes rough words with smooth) that led
To such exchanges – simply the theorem
That shapes of women that appeal to men
Are strict and pre-determined. She and he
(So must have been her assumption) were exempt
From law, and she imagining also the
Perennial lure of beauty beneath contempt.

XXXII

The lime tree's fruit, with helicopter blade
To ensure its scattering, swivels down,
The ancient pawnbroker's sign in miniature.
It startles her, sitting in sunlight – like
The tiny warnings once unseasonably
Falling from the blue into a happiness
That subsequent October-like devastation
Turned into grief.
It seems a legend now,
When even autumn's fragility was part
Of a robust commingling of life and art,
With waiting winter merely signalling
The sleeping seed under a springing heel –
Humans with every month in which to sing,
And art no more desirous than the real.

XXXIII

She thought him the superior at first –
Astounding time of the genius of youth,
Which is to believe as well as state the truth,
However best turns later into worst.

– Partly because he was her rescuer.
From what? All kinds of ill, most past recall,
Supplanted by a set it looks will all
Endure till her demise, and gather more.

She wakes and finds the bedroom curtains lit,
And thinks about the content of her dreams.
The house, still, will remain so till she stirs.

Among the rest, her daemon also quit,
And only ever comes visiting, it seems,
In these half-fathomed Brontëan nights of hers.

XXXIV

First, the unloading of her woes on him,
Then the discovery of the griefs he bore –
Which his lent strength enabled her to share.
Nothing much gathered by the brothers Grimm
Excelled the happy outcome of this start.
And as for their two fames – well, either one
Seemed fed by the other. But then, later, stones
Instead of kids rumbled beneath her heart.

As much because of her now slatternly ways
As tenderness to life, the spider stays
Inviolate indoors. How could she change,
Somewhere in the unfolding of the tale,
To a persona it was plain must fail,
Condemned for ever to the kitchen-range?

XXXV

Yet in the autumn life seems specially
Abundant – dancing flies in sunlight, grubs
Dangling on strings, and cobwebs netting shrubs.
The human must respond, and does – though she
Counts it a season towards eternity,
Despite the absence in her world of terror
More than an extra wrinkle in the mirror,
Or twinge she may ascribe to malignancy.

The final wars to come! Moon shining down
On an unlighted, empty earth – a super
Blackout of the kind her childhood knew!

But this may only be a plot on paper,
And nothing worse for her than withering brown,
Even backed sometimes by cerulean blue.

XXXVI

She criticized his verse before his nose.
That is, she saw first she'd been overawed
By talent: profile joined it later on.
Does admiration of the flesh depend
Upon the mind within it, in the end?
The question's like: can bad men write good prose?
To find the trochees and iambics flawed
Prepared her for discovering love had gone.

Epochs of art even by middle-age
Are quite discernible, let alone those of love.
It only needs the clumsy, old-fashioned glove
To be removed, bare fingers turn the page
To a clean place, and suddenly everyone
Is writing like Wagner or Alfred Tennyson.

XXXVII

She sees the spider scurry from the rain
That makes webs tremble. Which purveys the truth –
First or third person, middle-age or youth?
The ancient armies of remorse or pain
Invade her resisting memory once again –
The darling sibling's childhood death somehow
She might have avoided; or the recent now,
When the loving word stayed frozen in the brain.

The events of nature like those of history
Appal their participants; no comfort that
The ruined house is left bediamonded
(Except to impersonal poets who have shed
Their egotism – even what life is at –
In the mad servitude to artistry.)

XXXVIII

The verses that she wrote to him seem now
Quite metaphysical: it strikes her how
Already at such time she was preparing
For the elusive element in caring
That most endures. But who will see through those
Items marmoreal; generalized Rialtos;
Specified vegetation, mainly flowers;
Heraldry, insect life, and even giaours?

The naked moon in all its shapes astounds.
No wonder he worshipped her several names; great wounds
The goddess suffering at neglected shrines.
These later days she easily confines
Her inspiration to the physical –
The countenance's craters lit by old Sol.

XXXIX

She can remember what she wore at times
Happy and unhappy, trivial or tragic –
Matters more apt for prose, perhaps, than rhymes:
The feminine earthbound, underplaying magic.
What he forgot was rather more than ties
And shirts. But who's to judge the quality
Of celebration? As Proust said, nothing dies
That has survived. And each day she is free
To root back in her wardrobe, or go out
To buy a set of memories from a shop
(Though her experience is that a curious doubt
Attends new apparel). Connections never stop.
The assured symphonic period ends; begins
The works for cello, viola, violins.

XL

The quarto compositor's misprint or misreading –
'Crulentious' – rather insinuates what she feels
About her life: vague animosity.

How often in Eliza's reign the bleeding
Of humankind in verse! The comic heals
As best it can the wounds of Acts Five and Three.
But in her own day only the actual
Participants in tyrannies and wars
Appear to be entitled so to write –
Women confined to the girlish or shrewish role,
As scullions must stick to kitchen chores.
The mere perusers of tragedies may indite
Only such detail as a dead leaf blown
Indoors seems a map of some far, desert zone.

XLI

The heroines of Shakespeare: products merely
Of masculine imagination – thus
It seems to her amidst her ruined life,
Despite the dramas' images being severely
Focused on gardens, dogs, the daily round.
She used to think: suppose I woke and found
He had returned? But utterly ludicrous
To contemplate herself a Julio
Romano sixteen years had lined to no
Effect, save to make a more alluring wife.

The daughter who hid her love! Her hatred, rather.
All men are Lears. And yet, and yet – a tear
Started when mortal illness felled her father:
Hard woman's tender heart; strong man's great fear.

XLII

No doubt she could have similarly wept
For the already absent, traitorous spouse.
But now she merely tries to keep mind swept
Of demons, like the dust inside the house.

A spider, hanging bat-like, waits in furs
Through showers and shine to parcel up the flies,
Ending the little lives that might be hers.

Despite its range of beaded complexities,
The web's not there for any human joy.
Dusk coming on, the spider tight-ropes to
Any trapped small fry. She recalls the boy,
As she still often does, the sibling who
Dies in her infancy and his, and haunted
Those of her own, with terror of the enchanted.

XLIII

Life echoes life: husband and father, son
And brother. Through her unshared bedroom ceiling
Water seeps slowly from a faulty run
Of tank and pipe. For like subconscious feeling,
There's brought into a house the pressure of
Entire lacustrine systems. All the past!
Such utter rot, the primacy of love –
Unless self-love, alone the kind that lasts.

And so a man invades her solitude,
To screw the super-ego tight. There spill
Out now mere intimations of the nude
Body of earthly forces: the success
Of insects, say – the external cuticle;
1780: water equals gas.

XLIV

A sphere of gold, a mile in diameter:
If such existed, nature's laws would still
Accommodate it – so she read somewhere.
It follows maniacs abound, among
Whom she would class clandestine adulterers.
Sometimes she wonders if he might be ill,
Before remembering she need no longer care –
The family's end, an end of right and wrong.

She thinks: I could have loved into old age –
A confidence unlikely to be tested.
Long, long ago she wrote an immortal page

And numbered herself among the apple-breasted.
Save in mad kings, how comic-futile rage
Against the rung where the Creator rested!